To: _____

From: _____

Be Like Me from A to Z

Break Barriers and Achieve Your Dreams

Words By:
Debra Alexander, Julian Alexander,
Kaye Craft, Allyson Martinez

Illustrations by: Alison Hamilton

FOREWORD

This book invites you on a journey into the heart of diversity and to learn more about the Black people who, both in the past and today, have fought to break barriers, create benefits, achieve dreams, and make paths forward for all people.

The people you will meet in these pages come from all walks of life, different points in history and the present, and all ages. What connects them (and hopefully you to them) is that they pushed through doubt, fear, racism and lack of opportunity or access to turn those challenges into opportunities and to realize their dreams. As a result of that courage and determination, they transformed not only themselves but also the world we live in. We hope this book inspires you to start to live a life without limitations, whether those barriers come from the world outside or within you.

Take a look, enjoy the read, and see the many possibilities that exist for you in the portraits that follow.

A AMAZONS OF DAHOMEY

The Amazons came
from African Benin.
Fierce warriors, strong fighters,
inspiring women.

BLACK LIVES MATTER

We hear 'Black Lives Matter' ring through different nations. A unified chant drowns out discrimination.

Patrisse Cullors

Alicia Garza

Opal Tometi

#BLACKLIVESMATTER
#BLACKLIVESMATTER
#BLACKLIVESMATTER

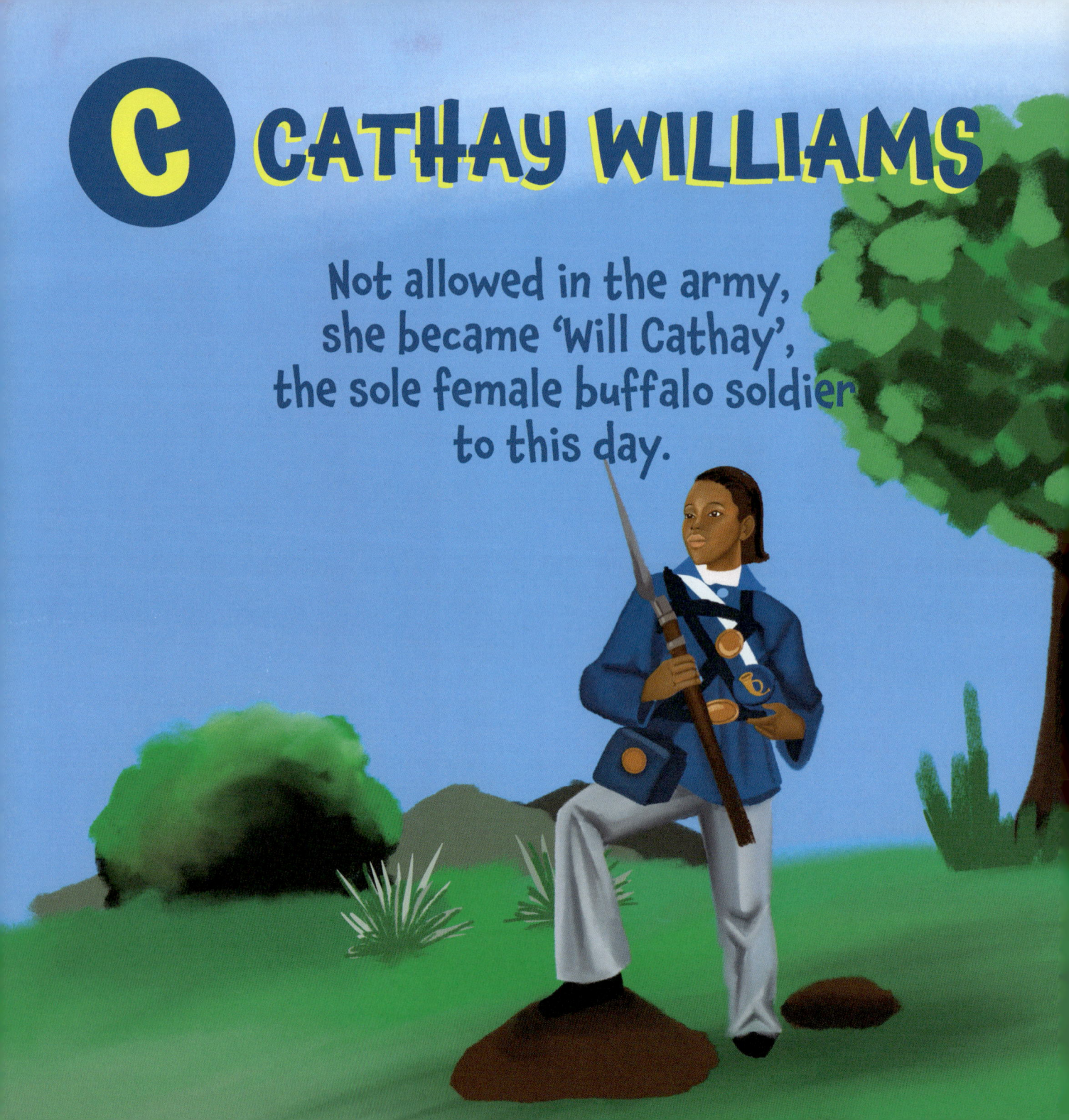

DASIA TAYLOR D

Healthcare is advanced by this young brilliant girl.
Inspiring inventions, saving lives around the world.

ELLA BAKER

She built up a movement
working hard out of sight,
Ella Baker was key
to all our Civil Rights.

FREEDOM

You're free to decide
just what you want to be
– the options are
endless, so repeat, 'This is ME!'

G AMANDA GORMAN

She owned the world's stage
aged just twenty-two.
Her poems wield power
with words heartfelt and true.

MATTHEW HENSEN

The race to the North Pole was on,
men moved fast.
Matthew Henson and Peary
were up for the task.

1 ISRA HIRSI

An environmental activist,
she works to save the planet
she's loud and clear on climate change
and young people now demand it.

SAVE THE PLANET

JOCKO GRAVES

In the harsh winter storm,
Jocko Graves remained calm.
Giving life up for light,
keeping George Washington safe
from harm.

K KETANJI BROWN JACKSON

That no Supreme Court Justice looked like her was no mystery.
So KBJ stood up and changed history.

NIKOLE HANNAH-JONES

She brought truth to light
And uncovered the facts
of 1619
And of slavery's bad acts.

BARACK & MICHELLE OBAMA

The Obamas showed the world what could be: 'Yes we can!' Chicago to DC, they brought Hope to the land.

PAUL ROBESON

Activist, attorney, athlete, singer and actor, Robeson showed what it meant to have the X-factor.

Q QUEEN CHARLOTTE

The young German princess who made quite a scene. Congolese ancestry made her Britain's first Black Queen.

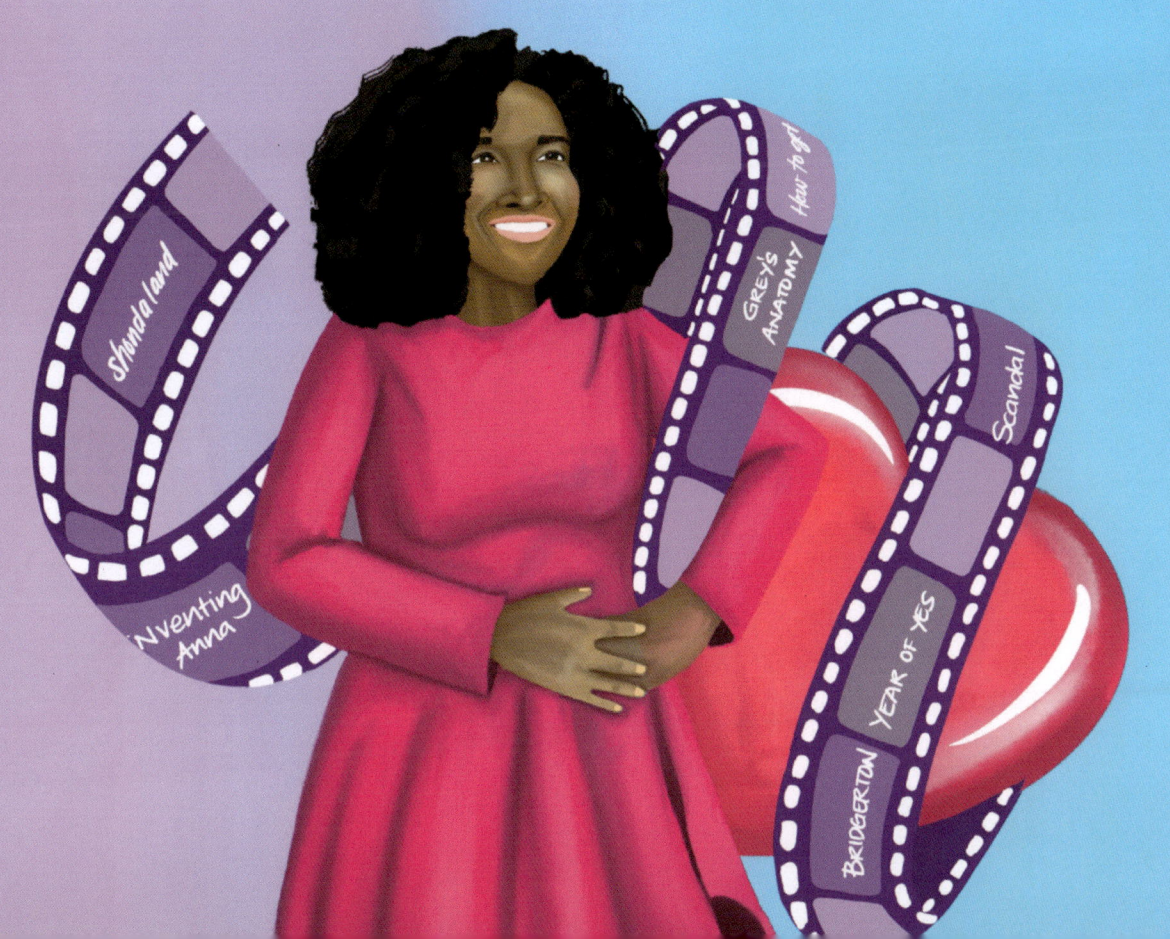

S IDDRIS SANDU

This 16 year old genius made new apps from his home. Now the biggest tech giants want those apps on their phones!

MIKAILA ULMER

With a fresh family twist on the lemonade stand, Mikaila uses bees to lend nature a hand.

VALERIE THOMAS

This inventor and scientist
deserves to be known,
Her breakthroughs are why
we take snaps with our phones!

M'LIS WARD

She broke all the boundaries and soared through the sky, so be like M'Lis Ward: **dream big and aim high!**

MALCOLM X

In our everyday lives
we feel the effects,
of the Civil Right Leader,
the great Malcolm X.

Y

YORK

The new-purchased West needed to be explored, but York's contribution cannot be ignored.

ZORA NEALE HURSTON

With everyday stories
about you and me,
She lifted Black people
for the whole world to see.

NOTES

AMAZONS OF DAHOMEY (1600s — late 1800s) — were a fierce group of female warriors in the kingdom of Dahomey. The fact that Dahomey's female warriors fought for their monarch and nation, even to the point of death, was what set them apart from other cultures' female soldiers. Today, the fearless Amazons of Dahomey are forever remembered as they inspired the Dora Milaje of Wakanda in the movie, Black Panther.

BLACK LIVES MATTER (b. 2013) — BLM is an anti-racism movement. It was born in 2013 following the deaths of Trayvon Martin, Rekia Boyd, and others at the hands of the police, and the acquittals of those responsible. Social media made these deaths and the protests that followed public and impactful. This energy was harnessed by 3 Black community activists, Patrisse Cullors, Alicia Garza, and Opal Tometi, as they formed the Black Lives Matter Network, an online movement to organize activists around shared goals of eradicating white supremacy and building local power for Black communities. BLM is also driven by a strong sense of allyship, offering White people ways to understand privilege and help overcome racism. 'Black Lives Matter' has now become a call to action for people worldwide, demanding that they unite in mass protest for racial equality and justice.

CATHAY WILLIAMS (b. 1844 — d. 1893) — Born into slavery, Cathay Williams was one of hundreds of women who were made to work as cooks, nurses or washerwomen in the early stages of the Civil War. In 1866, she took the name 'Will Cathay' and volunteered as a man, becoming the first Black woman to enlist in the army, and the only woman amongst the legendary 'Buffalo Soldiers,' the first African-American regiment in US military history. She remained undetected for some time, but unfortunately, her health worsened and eventually, a surgeon realized she was a woman. She was made to leave the army, and later requested a disability pension that could help pay for medical treatments. This pension was denied, and she passed away soon after. We remember her story and honor her role amongst the Buffalo Soldiers and her service to our country.

DASIA TAYLOR (b. 2004) — Dasia Taylor was only 17 when she came up with an invention that would save people's lives, using beetroots! In 2019, Dasia had the brilliant idea to apply the vegetable's properties in medicine. Thanks to her knowledge of science and her curiosity, she discovered that beets change color depending on the pH level of their environment. A bright red beet will turn dark purple if the pH level is at a nine. This specific level also means that there's an infection, which could lead to serious problems if not detected. With that in mind, Dasia thought of using beetroot dye on sutures so that people who had recently had surgery could tell if their wound was infected by the thread changing color.

ELLA BAKER (b. 1903 — d. 1986) — Ella Baker, known as the Mother of the Civil Rights Movement, is not as well-known as others such as

Martin Luther King, Jr. and Malcolm X. Most of her battles for the cause unfolded behind the scenes. From the 1940s, Ella spent many years building solid bases for the movement by recruiting people, raising money, and organizing meetings. It was a dangerous job for a young black woman. Many of the changes created by the Civil Rights Movement, over five decades, were driven by the hopes and dreams of Ella Baker.

FREEDOM — At its heart, freedom is about having the equal rights and equal access that enable each of us to be valued for who we are and what we bring. Enslaved people did not have freedom. People fought hard for freedom and we must continue to protect the right to freedom for everyone.

AMANDA GORMAN (b. 1998) — Amanda Gorman, an African-American, was named as the first National Youth Poet Laureate and has become one of America's most prominent poets and activists. She read her poem, *The Hill We Climb*, at the inauguration of President Joe Biden in 2021. Her message of accountability and responsibility for our freedoms captured people's hearts and minds across the world.

MATTHEW HENSON (b. 1866 — d. 1955) — Matthew Henson, along with expedition leader, Robert Peary, took part in the groundbreaking effort to be the first explorers to reach the North Pole. They were helped by the Inuit people on this grueling trek across the Arctic landscape. Henson showed his grit and became the first to claim the Pole. His incredible achievement went unrecognized because of racial prejudice against African-Americans.

ISRA HIRSI (b. 2003) — "You are never too young to fight for your beliefs." This is the message that Isra Hirsi, a young African-American and Black Muslim, sent to millions as she advocated and fought for climate change. She was in high school when she took a stand and organized student-led School Strikes for Climate. She continues to advocate for the voices of youth to be heard. She co-founded the U.S. Youth Climate Strike and has won several awards for environmental activism.

JOCKO GRAVES (Unknown) — Jocko Graves was only 12 years old when he joined his enslaved father to serve George Washington during the American Revolutionary War. On the night of December 26, 1776, Jocko waited for hours by the Delaware River for Washington's return. Though cold and alone, he held the reins of Washington's horse and a lantern to guide the way. That is how Washington found Jocko; he had frozen to death. Washington had a statue made to honor Jocko. These statues became popular throughout the South. The history they represent about the young, brave, Black boy, who gave his life for America's freedom, is not well known.

KETANJI BROWN JACKSON (b. 1970) — "My family went from segregation to the Supreme Court in one generation!" These words come from Ketanji Brown Jackson, the first African-American woman Supreme Court Justice. Being appointed to the highest court in the U.S. is a huge achievement for anyone and is a testament to her success in breaking barriers all along the way. She brings an unparalleled depth and breadth of experience to the Court.

HENRIETTA LACKS (b. 1920 — d. 1951) — Her headstone reads, "Here lies Henrietta Lacks (HeLa). Her immortal cells will continue to help (humankind) forever." The discovery of the unflagging replication rate of her cells made possible lifesaving research that could not have been conducted previously. This opened the door to previously impossible disease testing and allowed significant medical advancements in countless ways, ranging from Polio to HIV to Ebola to Parkinson's. It was not until 1975, after two decades, that the Lacks family learned about the remarkable properties of HeLa tissues and their worldwide use and continuing benefits.

MARSHA P JOHNSON (b.1945 — d.1992) — Born Malcolm Michaels, Jr., Marsha P. Johnson referred to herself as "gay, transvestite and Queen" at a time when the term "transgender" was not in common use. She is celebrated for her pivotal role in the Stonewall Uprising. This event was an act of resistance to the police harassment and violence against the LGBTQ+ community. Marsha continued to make a positive difference in the LGBTQ+ community as a founding member of the Gay Liberation Front and the Street Transvestite Action Revolutionaries, and joined ACT UP as an activist against AIDS. Today, June is Pride month in the U.S. which honors the 1969 Stonewall riots and works to achieve equal justice and equal opportunity for LGBTQ+ Americans.

NIKOLE HANNAH-JONES (b. 1976) — "I see my work as forcing us to confront hypocrisy, forcing us to confront the truth that we would rather ignore." Nikole Hannah-Jones is an African-American journalist, university professor, and Pulitzer Prize-winning reporter covering racial injustice for the New York Times Magazine. She created the landmark 1619 Project which helped to reframe the way we understand the history and legacy of slavery in the U.S., and the contributions of African-Americans.

BARACK OBAMA (b. 1961) AND MICHELLE OBAMA — (b. 1964) — The Obamas are celebrated for becoming the first African-American President and First Lady of the United States. Barack Obama had a mixed race experience growing up as the son of a Black Kenyan father and a White American mother, and being partly raised by White grandparents in Hawaii. His early experiences as a community organizer in Chicago influenced his social change agenda as President. He signed many landmark bills into law including the Affordable Health Care Act for all Americans. Michelle and Barack Obama met when he interned at the law firm where she worked as an attorney. As First Lady, she served as a role model for women and worked as an advocate for poverty awareness, education, physical activity and healthy eating. She supported American designers and is considered a fashion icon. Their legacy and influence are global and indelible.

PAUL ROBESON (b. 1898 — d. 1976) — Paul Robeson had many achievements. He was a stage and film actor, bass baritone concert artist, professional football player, activist and lawyer. He used his various platforms to fight against racial injustice. He courted disdain and public controversy for most of his career as a staunch advocate for human rights.

QUEEN CHARLOTTE (b. 1744 — d. 1818) — Queen Charlotte was a German Princess who married King George III of England in 1761. Her Congolese ancestry led contemporaries at the time to comment on her African features and appearance. They had 15 children and among her most famous progeny are her granddaughter Queen Victoria and her great-great-great granddaughter Queen Elizabeth II. When King George was determined to be severely mentally ill, the Prince of Wales was declared Regent (at only 5 years old) while his mother, Queen Charlotte was his guardian and thus very influential in ruling England. This is among the reasons that Queen Charlotte is sometimes referred to as England's first Black Queen. Many early American cities and institutions, such as Charlotte, NC and Charlottesville, VA, were named for her without recognizing her Black ancestry.

SHONDA RHIMES (b. 1970) — Shonda Rhimes Is an African-American television screenwriter, producer and author. She's best known for her work in series such as Grey's Anatomy, Private Practice, Scandal, How to Get Away with Murder and Station 19. She's been named 3 times on the Time 100, Time Magazine's annual list of the 100 most influential people in the world.

IDDRIS SANDU — (b. 1997) Iddris Sandu is a tech genius. He was born in Ghana and emigrated to Los Angeles, California with his family when he was 3 years old. In middle school he taught himself how to code using resources from the local public library. At 15, he designed an app that helped his classmates access learning tools more easily. It was this app that brought him national acclaim. President Obama granted him the Honorary Presidential Scholar Award. He created the world's first smart retail store experience with the late Nipsey Hussle. He's partnered with Kanye West, Jaden Smith and Virgil Abloh and has collaborated with large companies including Uber, Instagram, Adidas, Apple and Google.

BISHOP DESMOND TUTU (b. 1931 — d. 2021) — Desmond Tutu was a South African Anglican bishop and theologian, known for his work as an anti-apartheid and human rights activist. He was the first Black African to become both the Bishop of Johannesburg and the Archbishop of Cape Town. His words and actions empowered people and urged them to fight against apartheid, but to do so with a humanity that they had been denied. As he famously said, "Forgiveness helps give people the resilience to survive and remain human in the face of all efforts to dehumanize them."

MIKAILA ULMER (b. 2004) — Mikaila Ulmer is an African-American entrepreneur who started a lemonade business when she was just 4 years old. She was inspired by her great-grandmother's 1940s flaxseed lemonade recipe to which she added honey from local beekeepers. Her company, Me and the Bees, now supplies more than 1500 stores nationwide, including Whole Foods, Kroger and the Fresh Market. As part of her social consciousness, Mikaila donates 10% of her profits to charities concerned with saving bees. She shows us that age is no barrier to greatness and inspires us to BEE the change.

VALERIE THOMAS (b. 1943) —
Valerie Thomas is an African-American scientist and inventor who, while working for NASA, received a patent in 1980 for the illusion transmitter. It was later adapted for use in surgery as well as in television and video screens. She is best known for inventing a way to transmit three-dimensional images, or holograms, that appear real.

M'LIS WARD (Unconfirmed) — M'Lis Ward soared to the forefront of American history as the first African- American female captain in commercial aviation. After her service in the U.S. Air Force, she was employed by United Airlines. An avid golfer and basketball coach, she continues to be a role model for women interested in aviation.

MALCOLM X (b. 1925 - d. 1965) — While a young man in prison, Malcolm X joined the Nation of Islam and became a Black Muslim. He changed his name to Malcolm X to symbolize his unknown African ancestral surname while discarding the white slave master name of Little. He was a self-taught human rights activist and widely quoted orator. A controversial figure to many, Malcolm X is also widely celebrated for his pursuit of racial justice.

YORK (Unknown) — York was born into slavery and given to William Clark as a child. Clark brought York with him as part of his famous expedition with Meriwether Lewis. Lewis and Clark were charged with mapping the Northwest from the Mississippi River to the Pacific Ocean. Although enslaved, York was an integral part of the expedition's success. He could hunt, build shelter, tend to the sick, identify unknown plants and animals, as well as swim and navigate rivers. The indigenous people they encountered were curious about his skin color, paving the way for safe passage, which was crucial to the expedition's success. Despite the accolades to Lewis and Clark and other members of the expedition, Clark refused York's request to be freed and kept him enslaved. Although his role and contributions remained largely unknown for many years, today we remember, admire and celebrate York's achievements.

ZORA NEALE HURSTON (b. 1891 - d. 1960) —
Zora Neale Hurston grew up in the all-Black town of Eatonville, Florida. She was an anthropologist, author, filmmaker and folklorist. She wrote about her experiences growing up "colored" and her many works revolved around African-American culture including legends, Black mythology, and folklore. She was a central figure of the Harlem Renaissance. Her best known novel is *Their Eyes Were Watching God*. She became a role model for African-American writers, lifting the voices of Black people for all the world to hear.

ACKNOWLEDGMENTS

Chris Parker
for his editorial input and review.

Research input from:

Rebecca Craft Felder
(Early Childhood Educator)

Kaydence Moore
(10 years old)

Makaylah Lee
(9 years old)

Tanner Buchanan
(8 years old)

Bishop Moore
(12 years old)

Harper Buchanan
(7 years old)

Dear Wonderful, Sweet, Amazing Children (and Adults),

Diversity Decoded is a Black-owned, multi-generational family business. We explore the many dimensions of diversity, equity, and inclusion in order to make the information and materials available and accessible to everyone.

We hope the amazing people in this book inspire you to break through barriers and achieve your dreams.

With GRATITUDE,
Julian, Allyson, Debra, Kaye

Julian Alexander, son of entrepreneurs, is a filmmaker and educator. He has a passion for new media and alternative storytelling methods that explore intersectionality, inclusivity, and cultural borders. When he is not leading a film set, Julian is leading a classroom at the University of East London. His brand JulianShakesStory explores the use of hip-hop as a medium for engaging audiences in Shakespeare and other classics. Currently, he is a doctoral candidate researching the production of films using rap as the main storytelling instrument.

Allyson Martinez is the daughter of a long line of strong Black women (related either by blood or choice) who have served as models for what is possible despite the odds. Allyson is a practicing corporate attorney, a real estate broker, Co-Founder of Diversity Decoded and Co-Founder of Brooklyn Level Up, a non-profit community development corporation based in Brooklyn, NY. Her purpose is finding ways to use her passion, vision and creativity to make systemic social impact and create space for others in her community to be changemakers in the world.

Debra Alexander is a life long learner, the daughter of educators, Sidney and Beatrice Jordan Boose. Deb grew up in the segregated South where stories of Black achievers were few and little-known. She and her husband, Ben, are the principals of Alexander Consulting & Training, Inc., a thought leader in diversity awareness, equity mindedness and intentional inclusion. They are the creators of the M.E.E.T. on Common Ground diversity dynamics video series and products used by hundreds of organizations across the nation. She is one of the Principal Advisors to Diversity Decoded.

Kaye Craft is the child of Civil Rights activists and educators – Silas and Dorothye Craft. Conversations about race, equity and inclusion were served with most meals. Kaye is now a DEIB (diversity, equity, inclusion, and belonging) consultant and leadership coach who helps organizations shift their processes in the direction of relational culture in order to create equitable workplaces for all. Kaye is the President of K. Craft Associates, Inc and is based in Rockville, MD. She is one of the Principal Advisors to Diversity Decoded.

© 2023 Diversity Decoded, LLC.   All rights reserved.

ISBN: 979-8-9869267-0-4

No part of this publication may be reproduced, distributed, or transmitted in any form or by any means, including photocopying, recording, or other electronic or mechanical methods, without the prior written consent of the publisher, except in the case of brief quotation embodied in critical reviews and certain other noncommercial uses permitted by copyright law. Please honor the authors' work as you would your own. Thank you in advance for respecting out authors' rights.

The authors and publishing house hereby disclaim and do not assume liability for any injury, loss, damage, or disruption caused by errors or omissions, regardless of whether any errors or omissions result from negligence, accident, or any other cause.

For rights and permissions, please contact:
Diversity Decoded, LLC
info@diversitydecoded.com

Printed in Great Britain
by Amazon